Whistleblower
Ethics Regardless of the Outcome

Edward R. Lane

Copyright © 2018 Edward Roscoe Lane

All rights reserved. No part of this book may be reproduced or transmitted in any form or by any means, electronic or mechanical, including photocopying, recording or by any information storage and retrieval system, without permission in writing from the publisher.

Dr Roscoe Books –Ashville, AL
ISBN: 978-0-692-14588-3
Lane, Edward Roscoe
Whistleblower: Ethics Regardless of the Outcome | Edward Roscoe Lane
Edwardlane.org
Available Formats: eBook | Paperback
 distribution

Dedication

I have to start by thanking my wife Sena. Words really cannot express how much I appreciate her. Her love and support is what makes me complete. Proverbs 31:10 An excellent wife who can find. She is more precious than Jewels."

Thanks to my children Edron, Destiny and Evan for their encouragement during a very difficult time.

Thanks to my Mother Barbara Lane for every scripture she quoted and every prayer she prayed. Special thanks to my youngest son Evan for his assistance in writing this book. Without his help this book would not have been possible. Evan has not let his disability be an excuse to set goals and exceed in life. His never-give-up spirit and zest to live life to the fullest, no matter what obstacles he has faced, is what heroes are made of. He is my Hero.

About the Author

Edward Roscoe Lane is a dedicated professional with over thirty years of experience working in the criminal justice arena. Lane received his Master of Public Administration Degree from Jacksonville State University in Jacksonville, Alabama and worked for the Alabama Department of Corrections for over fourteen years before working with the Alabama Pardons and Parole Department for over seven years. He became the Director of Community Intensive Treatment for Youth (C.I.T.Y), a juvenile program operated by Central Alabama Community

College. Edward Lane was eventually thrust onto the National scene after a unanimous decision was issued by the United States Supreme Court in his favor. Lane's first Amendment case was a success for government and public servants who blow the whistle on corruption. With his unique background and training in human behavior and the criminal justice system Lane has distinguished himself as a one-of-a-kind real world expert on courage, integrity and ethics. In the face of adversity, his integrity has been unquestionable, and inspiring. He is a deeply spiritual person who attributes his success to faith.

Edward Lane has been married to his wife, Sena Lane, for thirty-five years. They have three children, who have all earned college degrees. He has one son-in-law, one daughter-in-law and three grandchildren. Mr. Lane currently lives in Ashville, Alabama where he enjoys fishing, hunting, cooking, gardening, running and most all spending time with his family.

Introduction

To some, doing the right thing may seem like a no-brainer. But when you're livelihood is hanging in the balance based on a decision you will need to make in your work life, doing what is right is not always easy. When faced with a monumental decision you might ask yourself, *"What harm will it do to look the other way?"* especially when looking the other way (or minding your own business) will help you keep your job. Coming from a low income, *albeit*, hardworking family from a small Alabama town, my career afforded my family with the opportunity to enjoy pleasures I was unable to experience growing up. I worked hard for my career and took pride in the opportunities it provided. My life experiences shaped me as a person, which made doing the right thing an easy decision for me. In doing the right thing, I don't mean ethics versus morals because ethics and morals relates to one's personal conduct and the ability to distinguish right from wrong. Ethics refers to a series of roles provided to an individual by an external source, e.g. their profession or religion. Morals refers to a person's principles regarding right and wrong. I was unwilling to do what was easy, and in the end, my career was damaged…almost irreparably.

> *Galatians 6:9 "…and let us not grow weary of doing good. In due season we will reap if we do not give up."*

Chapter One

I was born and raised in Eastaboga, a rural town in the heart of Alabama. There, my parents Sherman and Barbara Lane taught me and my siblings to work hard and insisted that we get an education. My mother instilled in us deep religious beliefs and also taught us to strive to be the best at whatever we chose to be in life. She would say, "If you are the floor sweeper, be the best floor sweeper they got," a quote I carried with me throughout my life.

The foundation had been laid early by my parents. They believed hard work, education, spirituality and morality was essential in developing their children into productive members of society.

My parents also impressed upon us that actions bring consequences and bad decisions render bad results. Of course, I would one day learn they were correct. As most young people do while growing up, I made some decisions that were bad and I got bad results.

Thankfully, I learned from my mistakes and grew from them. I grew in character and integrity. I learned early on that character is not only doing the right thing when no one is looking, but also doing the right thing when everyone is looking. It is a willingness to do the right thing even when the cost is more than you wish to pay.

"Integrity is doing the right thing even when no one is watching."
- Michael Josephson

The life lessons I learned in my youth prepared me for events that would test my faith, character, and integrity. I had no idea what the future would hold. I remember when Martin Luther King Jr., the famous civil rights activist and both Kennedys were assassinated. I remember my parents telling us you have to be twice as good as the white kids if you want to make it in this world. We were poor and didn't know it even though we grew up in a house so cold, in the winter time if you left a cup of water on the table it would freeze. Still, our hearts were full of warmth. In the summertime it was so hot you no longer realized just how hot it was. We worked in the fields, mostly for other people, doing what our parents told us without question. Our food source was what we grew and harvested. We raised our own hogs and chickens. We hunted for rabbits, squirrels, and raccoons. We were constantly reminded by our parents, that if we wanted better in life, we had to work for it, and remember to always do what is right. I recall at a young age working for this elderly white lady who lived not far from us. My mom would tell me, "Don't you pick up nothing that don't belong to you! If you find money laying in her yard, you leave it there." I would work for this little old lady cutting grass and doing other odd jobs. She would pay me five dollars after a full day of work. I was very young so, to me, five dollars felt like five hundred dollars.

Chapter Two

My first grade year in school was at Salem, a small all-black school located on what is now Speedway Boulevard, not far from Talladega Motor Speedway.

I remember walking to school. My parents were focused on my education, and insisted that I learn to read at an early age. I enjoyed reading because it allowed imagination to blossom. After the first grade, Salem, the little all black school was closed. I didn't know why back then, but later learned it was due to integration. I was sent to Eastaboga Junior High, an all-white school. There were less than 25 blacks at Eastaboga. Second grade was a difficult time but the transition went okay, I guess. My parents told to follow the rules and stay out of trouble. They preached that I was going to school because that is our key to a better life.

My time at Eastaboga went fast and it wasn't long before I was in the 9th grade and going to Lincoln High School. During those years, I worked almost every job you could imagine. I cleaned stalls, hauled hay, picked cotton, butchered hogs and cows, harvested watermelon, stripped sugar cane, picked corn, shucked corn, milked cows, cleaned gardens, the list goes on…. I also played youth league football and baseball. The work ethic instilled in me at an early age shone through. At Lincoln High School I continued to play sports while working summer jobs until I graduated. Hard work, education, integrity, character, and faith. Why faith you might ask? Faith in what I was taught would open doors of opportunity.

In the bible, James 2:14, *"What does it profit, my brethren, if someone says he has faith but does not have works?"*

You can believe something exists or that something will come to pass but if you do nothing to prepare yourself for moving toward your goal, it will never come to reality.

When I arrived at Lincoln High School, I was a mediocre student but I had faith. I continued to work hard and do the right thing. Profanity was absolutely forbidden in our house. My mom would not allow it at all. We could not even say the word "butt." We had to address men and women as Mr. and Mrs. We always had to say "Yes sir," "No sir," "Yes ma'am," "No ma'am," to adults, it didn't matter who they were. These rules were absolute. Mom didn't entertain any breach of manners in our household. There was no talking in church and you went to church every Sunday. Life has many ups and downs, but when you have an assignment on your life then certainly there is no weapon formed against you shall prosper. When I was young I once hurt my leg playing in the yard with other children. I do not remember a lot about that ordeal except that I was admitted into the hospital after my parents had already tried several home remedies. They took me to the doctor and he admitted me into the hospital due to a severe infection that had developed in my leg. My mother and father would take turns staying at the hospital with me and I can imagine they were traumatized when the doctor recommended amputating my leg in an effort to save my life. But God had other plans. My situation began to turn around and God healed me completely. I can assure you that when you have been predestined for a particular path, God will keep you until that appointment has been met.

Chapter Three

The determination to succeed and persevere during the most difficult times was instilled in us through everyday examples provided to us by how my parents lived their lives. My dad worked as a molder at a pipe shop in Anniston, AL and my mom worked at several different clothing factories in Calhoun and Talladega counties. Mom was cut from a different cloth as far as southern women. She would get up hours before work and cook breakfast, fix dad's lunch and then get ready to leave for work herself. When it was time to wash clothes, we had one of those wringer type washers that seemed to only work on its own accord. Mom would wash clothes in the hot summer and freezing winter but the job had to be done. When washing clothes in the winter time it was always a challenge due to the fact that the clothes would freeze by the time she could hang them on the clothesline. Dad always had a garden…at least, that is what he called it. My brother and I would argue that he was growing enough food to feed the world. Our job was to maintain a garden that that almost looked like large fields. We eventually realized it was my father's way of providing for his family. We would hunt game during the winter. I always enjoyed this, but I see now that hunting wasn't something for us to do, but also my father's way of providing for the family. During the summer months, my parents required us to find work. I often worked on some of the local farms hauling hay, cleaning stables, and cutting grass. My parents provided for us the very best they could and through it all instilled in me a determination to succeed against all odds. I remember one terrifying experience. I look back on it now, and laugh about it, but at the time it wasn't so funny. The primary source of heat for our house was a fireplace. This meant we had to cut fire wood. We had an old mule. His name was Ole George, who was about as stubborn as a mule could be. My dad used Ole George to plow the garden and pull the wagon that we hauled the firewood on. Most of the time, working with

Ole George was uneventful, especially when Dad was around. However, when Dad wasn't around, I'm almost certain that old mule knew it and acted accordingly. On this one particular time we went to cut firewood way deep in an area of the forest where the road was long and winding and barely passable. We worked hard to load the wagon and after it was loaded my Dad decided he was going to let me drive the wagon back to the house and unload it while he continued to cut wood. Once I got on that wagon and took the reins, I believe the old mule looked back and smiled. We started down the long winding road and just as we were out of my father's sight the old mule started acting up. I tried to get him under control but he wasn't having it. He started running and bucking down and around that winding trail of a road. There I was, bouncing around hollering and pulling on the reins trying to get that crazy mule under control, but he wasn't having it. When we finally reached the clearing into an open area there wasn't a stick of wood left on that wagon. Ole George didn't stop until we were back at the house. There I was…traumatized with that old mule looking like he had just had the best time of his life.

Psalm 23:4 yea, *though I walk through the valley of the shadow of death, I will fear no evil: for thou art with me; thy rod and thy staff they comfort me.*

Chapter Four

When building a foundation you must first pour the footing. When I graduated from Lincoln High School I was uncertain about what I wanted to do with my life. All I knew was Eastaboga, AL. Even though I played football and baseball, I wasn't sure about much of anything. I decided to go to college, but managed not to go too far from home. I went Jacksonville State University in Jacksonville, AL, where I also played as a walk-on football player. I didn't stay a walk-on football player long. With my newfound freedom; I did things I was never able to indulge in growing up. My grades suffered and I was placed on academic probation. Disappointed, my dad got me a job working as a brick masonry helper that summer. I believe it was the longest and hottest summer on record. We would leave before sunrise and not get home until almost dark. I had to give my mother all but a small portion of my paycheck each week. She was saving the money for me. She kept telling me, "You are going back to school this fall and you are going to get your lesson." After working as hard as I did that summer, when I went back to school that fall I was much more focused on doing what I needed to do. I eventually wanted more spending money and a car of my own. After I got back to school, my parents would give me twenty dollars and let me drive their 1966 Ford back and forth to school. I would also pack enough food so that I would have something to eat during the week. I made it through the school year but it was tough. When the school year ended, I was determined to find a job that wasn't as hot and hard as the masonry job I worked the previous summer. Instead, I went to the Holiday Inn in Oxford, AL on a tip that they were looking for a dishwasher. I met with the owner of the restaurant, a man named Jones. Mr. Jones hired me that day and I worked there until I graduated from college. After working as a dishwasher at the Holiday Inn for the final two and a half years of college, I couldn't wait to turn in my resignation. Not only was I graduating from college but without a job. After four years of college I was excited and apprehensive about what I was facing and starting a new chapter in life. In 1981, the economy was in bad shape and graduating with a degree in sociology and a minor in corrections didn't open many doors. I applied for jobs with little success. Moving back home with my parents, which was my only option until I could settle into a well-paying job, was a difficult task due to the fact I had come to enjoy my independence and my Mom had a strict curfew policy. If I failed to abide by the curfew policy I would be questioned by my Mom about what time I arrived home the previous night, knowing that she already knew the time of my arrival. I would give her my excuse however she would ask for my car keys and then say, "You will not be going anywhere tonight". I would hand over my car keys even though I was the one paying for it and here I was grounded after just graduating from college. I was struggling to find a job after graduating I had my car note and some other small bills that I was responsible for so after a couple of weeks I was able to find work at a small manufacturing plant that operated out of a building located on Talladega speedway boulevard. Here I was a college graduate making minimum wage working on an assembly line back at home in Eastaboga, Alabama .

> *Proverbs 16:9 A man's heart plans his way: but the lord directs his steps."*

I could not see it then but God was molding me and working on me then. I would check the help wanted adds daily until one day I saw an ad for help wanted for a company located in Sylacauga Alabama called the Sunshine center. It was a part of (ARC) Association for Retarded Citizens. I applied and was hired to help adults with disabilities live healthy and safely in their community. The job was fulfilling but the pay wasn't. I worked this job for about 2 years before I learned that the Alabama department of corrections was hiring and the opportunity to make better pay got me interested so I applied and was eventually hired.

Chapter Five

I started working for Alabama Department of Corrections, where I worked for over 14 years. I was apprehensive about working at a state prison but I was engaged to get married and I needed a better paying job. I remember the first day at St. Clair Correctional Facility I was nervous, scared and excited. I remember thinking you went through four years of college and here you are going from working on an assembly line at fireplace insert company to working at a state prison. The starting pay was $499 dollars every two weeks after taxes and insurance was deducted I would bring home about $380 dollars. I found myself having to do something I said I would never do again. I went back to washing dishes part-time at a local restaurant to help try to provide for myself and my new bride. I did what I had to do but I found myself questioning God.

> *Isiah 55:9, For my thoughts are not your thoughts, neither are your ways my ways, declares the LORD.*

For as the heavens are higher than the earth, so are my ways higher than your ways and my thoughts than your thoughts. Working at a maximum security state prison however did provide possibilities to move up through the ranks and subsequently make more money. I got promoted to corrections sergeant and a few years later to a correctional officer lieutenant. There were so many incidents that took place during my years working inside this maximum security prison such as escapes, stabbings, assaults and even a major riot where several of my coworkers were taking hostage and injured. The one incident that I was involved in that really made me consider quitting was during the time I worked as a corrections sergeant on the second shift. The state was in the process of starting a drug rehabilitation treatment on a large scale inside the state prison and decided to open the first treatment facility inside the prison where I worked. The opening of this treatment facility brought about a lot of internal changes at the prison and this caused greater stress in a place where the stress level was off the chart on a daily basis. It required that large groups of inmates had to be moved from different parts of the facility. On the day that the following incident took place my supervisor gave me a list of inmates that had to be moved from the treatment dorm to another part of the prison. I had another officer go with me to the treatment dorm and we advised the inmates whose names was on the list that they had to move. They were instructed to pack their property and would be moving to another dorm. They went to their prospective cells and within a few minutes this one particular inmate comes out of his cell which was located on the top tier with a large prison made shank (knife). The inmate shouted, "Lane you going to die tonight!" The officer that was with me jumps over the metal railing that surrounded the top tier and the inmate comes after me. I turn and ran towards the cubicle where the officer who operated it placed the cell block on lock down. The inmate was shouting for the other inmates to join in and assist him in taking my life. The other inmates would not join in and in what seemed like forever other officers arrived as the inmate approached me and all I had to keep him back was a broom handle. As the other officer arrived the inmate stopped his approach but continued to shout for the other inmates to join in with him. After he realized he wasn't going to get any help and several minutes of talking with him he threw down his weapon and gave up. We took him into custody and placed him in segregation. After the incident was over I remember my legs felt like jelly and I was shaking all over. It is a feeling that is hard to explain when someone comes after you with a weapon expressing their desire to take your life. The years working in this environment was what I see now as another step in the process of God molding and making me. During my time with DOC I was promoted to sergeant and then to lieutenant. I was second shift supervisor at a maximum security prison when I was hired with Alabama Pardons and Parole as a probation officer, then promoted to probation and parole supervision. I was then selected to be a (IPO) Institutional Parole

Officer. During my 14 years with DOC I went back to school and obtained a Master of Public Administration degree. My years of working for the state in the capacity of correctional officer supervisor and probation and parole officer supervisor also helped build a foundation of doing the right thing.

Chapter Six

I was an investigator when I was hired as the Director of C.I.T.Y, Community Intensive Treatment for Youth Programs. Scripture *Psalm* 37 and 23 states that the steps of a good man are ordered by the lord: and he delighted in his way. My life journey was moving towards destiny without my knowing it. Each event prepared me to become the director of C.I.T.Y Programs.

I learned about the job in the *Birmingham Newspaper* daily. I saw a classified ad in the Sunday paper that said the agency was looking for a director at CITY Programs. The job requirements seemed to fit my education and experience. I wasn't sure about submitting my resume for the position at first, but after thinking and praying about it, I decided to apply for the job, waiting until the deadline to apply for the position. Instead of mailing my resume, I walked into Central Alabama

Community College and delivered it personally. I stepped out on faith and trusted that what God had for me.

> *"Now faith is the substance of things hoped for, the evidence of thing not seen." Hebrews 11:1*

I wasn't notified by the personnel office at Central Alabama Community College about coming in for an interview until a few weeks later. In the meantime, I prepared for the interview and by researching what CITY was about and what it had to offer. I contacted a friend who lived near CITY Program's main office and had this person pick up any flyers or material that would give me some insight into what the program was about. I went to my first interview before a panel of employees. It was a tough interview and I was nervous.

> *"But without faith it is impossible please him, for he that cometh to god must believe that he is and that he is a rewarder of them that diligently seek him." Hebrews 11:6*

After a week of nervously anticipating the outcome, I was called for a second interview. I remember telling my wife that I might actually have a shot at this job. It felt great that they had considered me for the job enough to bring me in for a second interview. I continued my daily routine and waited. When I was contacted about a third interview, my excitement continued to build. Even though when I was contacted there was no indication of what the third interview would entail, but it felt great, knowing that I was a serious contender for the position. When I went to the third interview, I met with the acting president of Central Alabama Community College and the vice president of CACC, a state representative. I was offered the position at the end of the third interview, where I was informed that I had been chosen after a long interview process. I was so happy, I wanted to dance like the biblical David.

"And David danced before the Lord with all his might, and David was girded with a linen ephod."
- 2 Samuel 6:14

Chapter Seven

My journey to being hired as the state director of a juvenile youth program had been long and difficult. It was hard to contain my excitement as my new employers outlined problems plaguing CITY Programs. I was told that two of the programs had been selected to close at the end of the fiscal year. The programs that had been selected to close were the ones in Mobile as well as the one in Montgomery. The programs' closure was due to the fact that CITY Programs had been receiving a grant that was in excess of $600,000.00 for the past two or three years but had been denied the grant that year. The program involved utilizing grant money to hire employees and using the rest as part of their yearly operating budget. The employees who had been hired should have been hired contractually and that employment was contingent on the continuation of the grant money. However, this wasn't the case. This caused a problem resulting in the agency having to draft a RIF (Reduction in Force). I didn't want to lose two programs that I had been told not to worry about so I set out to save them. After I started, I met with my business manager, who was one of the most knowledgeable employees at CITY Programs and reviewed CITY policy, procedures, budget, and employees. I diligently searched for ways to keep the Mobile and Montgomery programs in operation. One of the discrepancies I found was in travel. We corrected this which was a plus. I then met with Dr. Thomas Corts who was chancellor of Alabama's two year college system at the time I was hired. I appealed to Dr. Corts for additional funding, hoping to keep all CITY Programs operational and he granted my request. I was successful in keeping all CITY sites open for that fiscal year. This was the time of the year when the State Legislative session was about to begin. I was working on submitting the fiscal year budget for next year while pulling together the ten programs in Alabama that spread out from Huntsville to Mobile, meeting with employees at each program site in an attempt to make programs more efficient. I also submitted a budget for the next fiscal year that included opening a new program in Florence, AL. With the help of State Senators Bobby Denton and Rodger Bedford, I was able to acquire the funding to open that program. The CITY Programs staff and I worked tirelessly to get the new program in Florence off the ground. This required finding a location and hiring the staff. Getting the program up and running was a tremendous task but through teamwork and faith we were successful. The opening of this program was one of my proudest accomplishments.

"Trust in the lord with all your heart and lean not on your on understanding; in all your ways submit to him, and he will make your paths straight." - Proverbs 3:5-6

The program was a good program. The young people who attended this program were successful in getting their GED, employment, and more importantly refraining from getting into more trouble in the community. The success rate of the young people who attended and the number of young kids who attended went up each year during the two and a half years that I was the director. I found that the CITY Programs had not had a conference in several years. I put together a team of employees to work on a conference for the CITY Programs employees. We were able to have a conference in Mobile where all the employees came together. The feedback from the employees proved that the conference was successful.

Chapter Eight

During my review of personnel, I learned one of my employees, Sue Schmitz, was a State Representative. My review of Sue Schmitz's work product was only one of the many things on my plate as the director of a state juvenile program. During my review, I found that she was being paid by CITY Programs, however, I could not find any work production that she was providing for the organization. I began to dig into her work productivity and started an investigation into her work performance. After asking around, and not finding any answers, I knew there was a major problem. I spoke with my business manager and the prior acting director who was now a Regional Coordinator for CITY Programs. They explained to me that this employee had been allowed to do what she was doing. At first, they didn't want to say more than that. I was eventually able to gather more information after reviewing a file I previously not had access to. It was obvious...Ms. Schmitz's employment with CITY was fraudulent. I presented my concerns to CITY Programs legal advisor and his legal advice made it clear that I needed to take some kind of action. The legal advisor gave me his opinion along with some advice on being careful with how I interacted with Ms. Schmitz due to her political status. I was already aware of this because my business manager and the acting director told me that Ms. Schmitz was someone who carried a lot of weight. As soon as I mentioned her name and what kind of work she was doing, or the lack thereof, I was warned about the possible trouble I was stirring up.

> 2 Timothy 1:7, "For God hath not give us the spirit of fear but of power and of love and of a sound mind."

I was compelled to resolve this problem rather than ignore it, especially when there was such a great need within our program for funding. I couldn't feign ignorance. I was determined to provide the kids we were working with the best chance at success and to also give the tax payers of this state the very best service we could provide and that meant, not wasting their tax dollars. I decided to discuss my concerns with Ms. Schmitz. When I contacted her, I explained who I was and that I was concerned about her duties and responsibilities. I told her that until I had a chance to meet with her and outline my expectations, that she was to report to the Huntsville CITY Programs site on a daily basis. I explained that there was an ongoing investigation into the two year college system and one of the areas they were looking at were legislators who held jobs but were not doing any work. I expressed concern about her job and that what she was providing for us looked rather suspicious. I explained to Ms. Schmitz that by her reporting to work every day like other employees, if any questions were raised, I would be able to point to what she was doing and where she was doing it at. I explained to Ms. Schmitz that not reporting to work on a daily basis or not providing a work product was not going to continue. She stated that she understood and that was the end of the conversation. I contacted the director of the

CITY program office in Huntsville and advised him that I had talked to Ms. Schmitz and she would start reporting to work that location. A couple of days later he called me and stated that Ms. Schmitz had come by his office and told him that she would not be able to report to work on a daily basis. She wanted to continue earning a salary while not reporting to work. I contacted Ms. Schmitz about why she would not be able to report to work on a daily basis. She then began to ask me if I knew how she got her job. I told her I didn't. She proceeded to tell me and then advised that she wanted to continue to do what she was doing. I later sent a certified letter to Ms. Schmitz advising her that I needed to meet with her at the main office for CITY Program in Talladega, AL. She reported to CITY main office in Talladega, AL at the scheduled time along with her Alabama Education Association (AEA) representative. When we met, prior to the meeting I advised my supervisor, who was the acting president of Central Alabama Community College (CACC) and CITY legal advisor that if Ms. Schmitz insisted on continuing to do what she was doing then I was going to terminate her contract. I was warned by both acting president and the legal advisor. I asked the business manager to sit in on the meeting, take notes and record the meeting so that there would be no misunderstanding about what was said and who said what. When the meeting was over I terminated Ms. Schmitz's contract. She was unwilling to report to work on a daily basis, much less provide us with a viable work product.

I am unsure how many weeks or months went by but eventually one day I received a call from an FBI agent asking questions about Sue Schmitz. I answered what questions I could but advised them that she no longer worked for CITY. They wanted to come to my office and talk to me and advised that they would be bringing a subpoena to get access to Ms. Schmitz personal file. After they met with me I was eventually subpoenaed to the Birmingham, AL Federal Court house in reference to a grand jury investigation of the two year college system and Ms. Schmitz. I went and met with the grand jury and told them what I knew about whatever they asked me. After the grand jury concluded I learned that Ms. Schmitz was being indicted. After she was indicted and a trial date was set I was subpoenaed to testify at her first trial. In my day to day operations as the director of CITY I would attend meetings of state school board and at the main office of Alabama Community Colleges. I was told by one of the attorneys for the Alabama Community College system that I had really taken a big chance on my career by doing what I had done in terminating Ms. Schmitz. One of the state school board members told me after one of the board meeting that I had taken a huge chance taking the director job at CITY because they had discussed doing away with CITY on more than one occasion. These warnings were a great concern to me but I was certain that I had done the right thing and actually hoped that the success of CITY since I had become the director would be what my performance would be based on.

Proverbs 15:3, "The eyes of the Lord are in every place, beholding the evil and the good."

The pressure of being the director of a program that was providing a safety net for so many young people was enough by itself. The added pressure of feeling that I could be terminated because of my decision to terminate an employee who wasn't doing what she was hired to do made things much more stressful. Along with that, the state's financial situation in the second year of my employment was really pushing me to the edge.

> *Proverbs 3:5, "Trust in the Lord with all thine hear and lean not unto thine own understanding."*

The governor called for proration during that year and this created a situation where I was told to prepare for a possible reduction in force (RIF). CITY was growing and had even received attention from the Chief Justice of the Alabama Supreme Court. She had called and requested a meeting with me in reference to CITY programs. There was a meeting with the Director of the Alabama Department of Youth Services. CITY Programs and success rate of the young people of the program didn't go unnoticed. It was a sweeping success. The help CITY provided young people who attended CITY is what made me continue on even though I was under so much pressure. The subpoena to testify at Sue Schmitz's trial wasn't something I looked forward to but when it arrived it was never a doubt in my mind about testifying. I arrived at the federal courthouse and testified as I was required to do in the first trial. The first trial ended in a hung jury. I continued to do my job with CITY trying to make sure that the program continued to provide the very best service we could for the kids we were serving. To me the citizens of Alabama deserve their hard earned tax dollars be utilized in positive professional way and not abused. The proration that was called by the governor had caused a serious financial situation with all state agencies and programs. I was working with my supervisor on putting together a RIF in case the financial problem got to a point that we would not be able to continue operating at the level we were originally funded even though we had already cut back drastically in every area we could without affecting the services we were providing. At the end of 2008, I was informed that I would begin reporting to my new supervisor Dr. Steven Franks. It was around the time that I heard that the federal government was possibly going to retry Sue Schmitz. I met Dr. Franks once before the end of the year in 2008 at a state school board meeting in Montgomery. I went in to Christmas break preparing for the 2009 legislative session and the possible RIF that was looming if tax receipts didn't pick up and the state's financial situation didn't improve. In January of 2009, when I returned to work it had been decided that the federal government was indeed, going to retry Sue Schmitz. After a couple of days of working in the New Year I was contacted by Dr. Franks stating he wanted to meet with me in my office in Talladega. He indicated he wanted to meet with me to discuss CITY operations since he didn't know how the program operated. He also indicated he wanted to be brought up to date on what work I had done on a possible RIF. On the day that I met with Dr. Franks I arrived at my office in Talladega thinking I was meeting to discuss CITY business. When I got there, CITY's business manager was already there. I spoke with her and asked where Dr. Franks was at since I noticed his car in the parking lot. She indicated she wasn't sure. However she told me that a regional coordinator whose office was located in Talladega had come by her office and made the statement, "I understand you have your marching order." I asked what she meant by that but she said she didn't know. Dr. Franks came to my office shortly after I spoke to the business manager. When he came in he made small talk with the office staff then he went into my office. After we got into my office we began to discuss the RIF and he informed me that a decision had been made to go ahead and proceed with the RIF. I was surprised since I was the director of CITY and had not been involved in the final decision. Dr. Franks informed me that the RIF would include about 27 employees. I then found out very quickly why I wasn't involved in the final RIF meetings. Dr. Franks told me that he had been told to let me go. He then preceded to hand me a notice of termination. He was trembling as he handed it to me. He told me to clean my desk and leave the building immediately. To tell you, I was in shock would be an understatement. I preceded to pack my stuff while trying to maintain my dignity. After packing my belongings I walked out of my office, but with my head held high. I spoke to the staff before I left. I told them it was my last day with CITY. When I spoke to the business manager she said she was sorry and that she only found out about my termination before I arrived but could not say anything when I came in. I asked that she send an email to staff at all sites advising that I was no longer employed with CITY Programs. Once I got into my car to I realized I left a ton of documentation in my office. But it was too late to retrieve it. I drove away from my office in shock, unsure of where my life would go from here. I waited before calling my wife. I wasn't sure how to tell her I had been fired from my job. The first phone call I made was to the CITY Programs retired attorney who had told me on more than one occasion to watch my back. I wanted to let him know that I had been terminated and to also see if he knew that they had decided to let me go since his wife was a state school board member. He indicated he knew nothing but stated he wasn't surprised. I called my wife and told her that I had been fired. This phone call was very hard. She was trying to be strong and assured me that we would be OK. She could tell I was upset. I was praying and crying as I drove home wondering how I would provide for my family.

Proverbs **22:22**, *"Rob not the poor, because he is poor, neither oppress the afflicted in the gate; for the Lord will plead their cause and spoil the soul of these that spoiled them."*

Chapter Nine

The day after my termination I received a call from a CITY employee who asked if I had been notified that all the employees who had received a letter the day before advising them they were being terminated were now notified to disregard these letters and return back to work. I had them send me a copy of the letter and advised them that I had not heard anything. I called the Department of Postsecondary Education Legal Office to ask about what I had heard. The attorney I spoke to told me she could not talk to me and hung up. I then called the Alabama Education Association (AEA) and informed them of what was going on and advised them that I needed legal representation. I also called the retirement systems to inquire about retirement paperwork. I received another subpoena a few weeks after I was terminated to testify in a second trial for Sue Schmitz. I was no longer working for CITY or the Alabama Department of postsecondary Education, but I went and testified in the second trial. Sue Schmitz was found guilty and was sentenced 30 months in federal prison. The fact that she was found guilty didn't change my situation at all, I was still without a job. I was able to retire since I had more than 25 years of service with the state of Alabama. I wasn't ready to retire nor did I want to at this time but I had no other option. I felt at this time I had my family to think about as I moved forward, my wife and kids depended on me to provide for them. I had two children in college and one child in high school. My youngest son was born with a muscle disorder called Myotubular Myopathy. He was in a wheelchair and had numerous medical problems. I had to maintain health insurance for my family so retirement would allow me to have some income and be able to continue our health insurance. The following days, weeks, and months were very difficult since my salary had been cut by more than half. I was notified by AEA that they would provide me with an attorney. I finally met with the attorney that was assigned to me several months after I had been without a job.

The attorney assigned to me was John Saxon. When I met with him I provided him with background information about my situation and provided him with all of the documents that I had in my possession in reference to my job and termination. Attorney Saxon listened to me and the details I provided and told me he would do what he could but my case would be a difficult one. I told him that if at all possible we needed to get my case into federal court if I was to have any chance of winning my job back. I told him that there was so much corruption in Alabama that I wasn't sure how deep the corruption went. I asked Saxon point blank if he was beyond being bought or corrupted. He assured me that he would fight for me with all the legal means he had available to him. He went to work on my case and was able to get the case into federal court in Birmingham. Unfortunately, the federal court in Birmingham ruled against me. To tell you that I was disappointed would be an understatement. All I had was my faith and I trusted that if it was God's will then I would have to accept my fate.

> *Hebrews 2:13, "And again, I will put my trust in him and again behold I and the children which God hath given me." James 1:3, "knowing this, that the trying of your faith worketh patience."*

These Scriptures and many others kept me strong during these difficult times. Eventually, I received a call from an attorney at the National Education Association office stating that they had looked at my case and wanted to appeal it to the 11th circuit court in Atlanta, GA. The federal appeals court in Atlanta asked us to mediate the case. We attempted to mediate but were unable to get anywhere in mediation. The State's offer was ridiculous and money was really not the point of my complaint. I had been fired (terminated) from a job that I had worked hard to make successful. Everything I did during my tenure as director improved the program. The statistics and the work I had done spoke for itself. It was the principle more than anything.

After the mediation process proved unsuccessful, the federal appeals court gave us their ruling and they ruled against me. Again, I was disappointed by the ruling but I was ok because I was able to sleep at night knowing that I had stood by my principles. There is an old saying that if a person will not stand for something, they will fall for anything.

Chapter Ten

By the time the federal appeals court in Atlanta heard my case, I had landed a job with the Department of Defense. I was hired at Anniston Army Depot as a police officer. This wasn't the job I wanted but it ended up being a blessing to me and my family. It was a requirement that if you could not get a waiver to go to the federal police academy you would have to attend the academy. I was unable to get a waiver and had to go to the academy in Fort Leonard Wood, Missouri. The year I had to go was the same year my youngest son with the disability was graduating high school. I decided to go ahead and go to the police academy early because I didn't want to take a chance on being sent during graduation. I was sent in February of that year to Missouri where the weather can be very difficult due to so much snow. The academy was nine weeks long. It was rather uneventful except for one of my trips back to the academy when it snowed. I would drive home every weekend from Missouri. A one way trip from the academy was about 11 hours. I would leave on Friday after class arrive home early Saturday morning then drive back on Sunday arriving back Sunday night. The trips were long and hard but it was worth it to be with my family. This one particular weekend, I came home the weather service was predicting a snowstorm in Missouri. I left home early Sunday morning hoping I would make it back to the academy before the storm hit. I was unsuccessful in my efforts. I ran into the worst snowstorm I had ever seen in my life. I could hardly see and I was in an area that I was unfamiliar with. I pushed on because we had been told that it was our responsibility to get to class on time every day. I almost lost control of my car a few times. The 11 hours that it had taken me during prior trips now turned into over 16 hours before I made it back to the barracks where we stayed. I was happy that I made it but there was a part of me that was upset about everything I endured.

> *Romans 5:3, "And no only so, but we glory in tribulations also; knowing that tribulation worketh patience."*

When I was contacted by the National Education Association's attorney, advising me that there was a law firm out of Washington that wanted to talk to me about appealing my case to the United States Supreme Court, I was excited. I told the attorney that I would be happy to talk to this law firm. I was contacted by an attorney from Goldstein and Russell. I had never heard of this law firm but was happy that they wanted to represent me. In my mind it was just another sign that doors were being opened and there was something special going on with my case. The attorney that was assigned to my case by Goldstein and Russell P.C. Attorney Tejinder Singh who I learned had clerked for Judge Diana Matz on the US Court of Appeals for the fourth circuit. He is a graduate of Harvard Law School. A petition was presented to the US Supreme Court on my behalf by Attorney Singh. He advised me that the petition to the court would be one of the many but told me that the petition was a very good argument on my behalf. He advised that the only thing to do now was sit and wait for the court to decide if they would even consider my petition. (Put Proceedings and Orders) *from scotusblog.com.

This picture was taken April 28, 2014 the day Oral Arguments was conducted in my case by my Attorney TEjinder Singh. Attorney Singh is a Partner at Goldstein & Russell, P.C. . Attorney Singh and the Law firm did a tremendous job preparing and arguing my case before the Supreme Court. Attorney Singh can be contacted at

GOLDSTEIN & RUSSELL, P.C.
7475 Wisconsin Avenue
Suite 850
Bethesda, MD 20814
202-362-0636
Information@goldsteinrussell.com

Chapter Eleven

When I was notified by my attorney that my petition was granted I was excited beyond belief because I knew that just getting my petition granted was a big deal at the US Supreme Court. The anticipation of my case being heard by the Supreme Court was really something. Once I knew the date that the court would hear my case, I made the decision that I would be in court when my case was argued. To have a case heard by the US Supreme court was and is a very big deal. My wife and youngest son went with me to Washington to hear the oral arguments pertaining to my case. Sitting in court in front of the nine US Supreme Court Justices was a moment that you remember forever. Sitting in the United States Supreme Court listening to a case that bore your name was, in my mind, a miracle. The US Supreme Court receives approximately 10,000 petitions for a writ of certiorari each year. The court grants and only hears oral arguments in about 25 to 80 cases.

The entrance of the Supreme Court and the building was breathtaking. The building complex was constructed from gleaming white Vermont marble, almost blindingly reflective in the sunlight. Watching the Justices and listening to the attorneys during the trial left me reflecting on my life. I was so very blessed to just be in the court with my wife and son. I was so thankful for this moment and felt that this was truly a special event. When we returned to Alabama it was time to do what I had learned to do best throughout this entire process, wait.... I had to wait to hear what the court's opinion would be and months went by without word. I was working out on my treadmill at home when I received a message from Attorney Singh that the court had issued an opinion in my case. The news was good and not so good. The court ruled unanimously on my first amendment claim but ruled against me on the qualified immunity argument. When I received the message the joy that I felt was overwhelming. I was happy because I had been vindicated. The fight for me was about principle in the first place. I worked hard to make CITY Programs a first class state sponsored program that was helping children to become successful and overcome bad decisions that put their lives on a negative path.

Yes I was happy, though "happy" seems insufficient to describe how I really felt after waiting and fighting what appeared to be an impossible fight. I am reminded of a scripture in 2 Timothy 4: 10 -11 when Paul wrote *"At my first defense, no one came to stand by me but all deserted me."* However, during my darkest times, my wife, my kids, my mom, and other family members stood by me, prayed with me and for me. I found that when it appears as if every door has been closed and there is no way out that is when the answer will come. Attorneys calling and asking to represent you without charging a dime. If I would have had to pay for the legal representation I received my case would have went nowhere. Exodus 14:14 says, *"The LORD shall fight for you and you shall hold your peace."* Over the years, after I was wrongly terminated, I could not help but think about the many times when I have had to fight the forces of evil. When I was asked by a person of great power and authority to purchase a reading program from a company called *FastForward*. The cost of the program was far beyond what I could approve without following the state bid law requirements. When I was asked to contact a certain lobbyist to seek help for funding, that specific lobbyist later went to prison. I reported the request to my supervisor who in turn took me to speak with the chancellor of the Alabama community college system. After telling the chancellor what was going on, they stated they would speak to the person who made the request, because that person knew I was legally not allowed, to do what was asked. I later received a phone call from someone who claimed that they were the powerful person's assistant and wanted me to know that I would regret that I had said anything. I also thought about when I was contacted by a top official from the Department of Youth Services shortly after I became Director of CITY Programs. The person stated that they wanted to move CITY under their agency. However, they would not be able to bring along all of the current CITY employees. Despite being promised a job along with the employees who would be brought over, I refused because I didn't want to sell out the many employees who would lose their jobs. The people who were lobbying for this possible move no longer hold their positions. After winning in the United States Supreme Court, I was asked to appear on the Alabama public television show called Capitol Journal. They asked me for my final thoughts on the whole ordeal to which I stated, "There is a lot of corruption in this state." My statement has proven to be true on so many levels since I was terminated there have been several State of Alabama government officials who have been found guilty of corruption. I have moved on in my life knowing that even though I was DONE WRONG I was vindicated by the UNITED STATES SUPREME court.

ADDENDUM

State Representative Sue Schmitz Found Guilty

U.S Attorney's Office
February, 24, 2009

Northern District of Alabama (205) 244-2001

Fbi.gov
https://archives.fbi.gov/archives/birmingham/press-releases/2009/bh022409.htm

DECATUR, AL—SUZANNE L. SCHMITZ, 63, of Toney, Alabama, was found guilty today on 7 out of 8 counts of federal fraud charges. The verdict is announced today by U.S. Attorney Alice H. Martin; Acting Alabama Attorney General Richard J. Minor; Special Agent in Charge Carmen S. Adams, Federal Bureau of Investigation; and Inspector in Charge Martin Phanco, U.S. Postal Inspection Service.

In January, 2008, SCHMITZ was indicted on mail fraud and federal program fraud charges involving The Community Intensive Training for Youth ("CITY") Program in Huntsville.

The CITY Program operated in 10 locations throughout Alabama and sought to develop social, behavioral, and academic skills possessed by "at-risk" youth. Students were referred to CITY Program through the juvenile court system. Evidence presented at trial revealed that SCHMITZ held the title of "Program Coordinator for Community and External Affair," at the CITY Program from January 2003 to October 2006, and received approximately $177,251.82 in salary/benefits despite performing little to no work. During the time she was paid by the CITY Program, through its fiscal agent, Central Alabama Community College, Schmitz rarely went to her Huntsville office, performed virtually no services, generated virtually no work product and submitted false statements to CITY Program regarding the volume and nature of work that she was performing, all in an effort to continue to collect her salary and benefits.

"It is an important victory and speaks to the need for public servants to serve the public not their own interest," stated United States Attorney, Alice H. Martin. "My congratulations to the trial team and investigators who worked tirelessly to obtain justice."

"I am very pleased with the jury's verdict today. Ms. Schmitz violated a trust to which her constituents and all Alabama citizens should be entitled. All citizens have a right to expect their elected officials to serve honestly and ethically. Public officials are elected to serve the public, not exploit their position for personal gain," stated Richard Minor, Acting Alabama Attorney General.

"I am pleased with the decision handed down by the jury this afternoon. Let today's verdict send a message to any politician who would consider violating the public's trust. You will be investigated, prosecuted and pay for your crimes," stated Carmen S. Adams,

Special Agent in Charge, Federal Bureau of Investigation, Birmingham Field Division.

"The guilty verdict against Representative Schmitz illustrates that the public will not tolerate anyone using the Postal Service to further a fraud scheme, regardless of their position in the community," stated Martin Phanco, Inspector in Charge, United States Postal Inspection Service, Atlanta Division.

The investigation of this matter was conducted by law enforcement officers from the Federal Bureau of Investigation and United States Postal Inspection Service. Assistant United States Attorneys William C. Athanas and David Estes prosecuted the matter on behalf of the U.S. Government.

Most Dangerous Specimen of Employee Wins Again

By Tommy Eden

Alabamaatwork.com

In September 2006, Edward Lane accepted a probationary position as Director of Central Alabama Community College's Community Intensive Training for Youth Program, a program for at-risk youth in Alexander City, Alabama. Lane promptly audited the program's finances and discovered that then state representative Suzanne Schmitz was listed on the payroll but wasn't reporting for work and not otherwise performed tangible work for the program. Schmitz lived in Madison County but refused to report for work at the Huntsville campus.

When Lane raised his concerns about Schmitz internally, College President Steve Franks warned him that terminating Schmitz's

employment could have negative repercussions for both Lane and the College. Despite these warnings, Lane terminated Schmitz's employment for refusing to report to work.
Schmitz was eventually convicted of federal mail fraud and sentenced to 30 months imprisonment; 36 months of supervised release, 360 community service hours and pay back the $177,251.80 she received in public funds.

Within 90 days after Lane testified at Schmitz's first federal court trial, he was fired by College President Franks. Lane then filed a lawsuit claiming that his termination was in retaliation for his testimony given in the Schmitz case, in violation of his Free Speech First Amendment right.

On June 19, the United States Supreme Court held in a unanimous decision that Edward Lane should not have been denied First

Amendment protection, and fired, for his subpoenaed testimony that was a matter of public concern. The high court then sent the case back to the 11th Circuit Court of Appeals on the equitable relief and damages issues. On October 10, the 11th Circuit held that Lane may seek the equitable relief of reinstatement to his former position at Central Alabama Community College for the First Amendment violation. However, the Court did find that the 11th Amendment to the Constitution precludes an award of damages against the State of Alabama and the College President.

Common Sense Counsel: Edward Lane is a profile in courage whose 8 years of perseverance has been rewarded by the United States Supreme Court and now the 11th Circuit of Appeals. The Lane case deals with the most dangerous specimen of employee – the sacred (someone who engages in protected conduct then is retaliated against). Lane was a whistleblower and employers across America are playing millions in fines and verdicts every month to the Edward Lanes of this world. OSHA enforces 22 different whistleblower anti-retaliation federal laws from truck drivers to healthcare workers. Taking these 5 steps will help you avoid being the target of a whistleblower claim:

1) Prevent the whistle from being blown by putting in place ethics, no retaliation and harassment prevention policies in your handbook;

2) Regular training on your policies with documentation of attendance;

3) Conduct routine audits to tests compliance with polices;

4) Put in place a defensible reporting, investigative and response plan if allegations of wrongdoing surface; and

5) Praise the internal whistleblower instead of firing them.

Tommy Eden is a partner working out of the Constangy, Brooks & Smith, LLP offices in Opelika, AL and West Point, GA and a member of the ABA Section of Labor and Employment Law and serves on the Board of Directors for the East Alabama SHRM Chapter. He can be contacted at teden@constangy.com or 334-246-2901. Blog at www.alabamaatwork.com

Posted by Tommy Eden at 11:57 AM

Labels: Employee, Employers, OSHA, whistle blower

Fired Alabama hero shows need for Constitutional common sense clause
By John Archibald

Edward Lane ought to be an Alabama hero.

We should have pinned a medal on the guy. You know, special commendation for *doing the right thing.*

At a time when doing the right thing wasn't common.

The guy ran a program for troubled youth at Central Alabama Community College in Alexander City when the state's two-year college system was a hissing, spitting snake pit of corruption. Lane had the nerve, the audacity, as it turned out, to demand to know exactly what then-State Rep. Sue Schmitz was doing to earn the almost $50,000-a-year she scammed in salary.

He found she was doing nothing. Nada. It was a phony gig, a get-paid-to-be-our –pal setup for legislators. She was just another lawmaker – a third of the

Statehouse had jobs of one sort or another in the two-year system at the time – nuzzling unapologetically up to the trough.

And giving nothing in return.

So in 2006 Lane fired her. He fired her despite threats and indignation, despite pressure and the shaking of all those political heads. He told Schmitz not to come back. Even as Schmitz, according to court records, vowed to get him back. If he came to the Legislature looking for money for those kids again, she'd simply tell him "you're fired."

So there.

But Lane stood his ground.

He was soon subpoenaed by the FBI, so he testified – truthfully -- before a grand jury.

He was subpoenaed again, so he testified– truthfully -- in Schmitz' criminal trial.

Schmitz went off to prison, where she served 27 months on federal mail fraud and theft charges before being released in 2012.

But Lane didn't get a medal. Nope. He got a pink slip.

He was unceremoniously fired for speaking up and for telling the truth. He helped clean up that snake-infested two-year-college pit for the benefit of all Alabamians. And this is what he got.

The ax.

He sued for his job, but lower courts ruled against him, saying his testimony wasn't protected free speech because he was testifying as a public college employee, not as a regular citizen.

So he had no Constitutional protection.

"That Lane testified about his official activities pursuant to a subpoena and in the litigation context, in and of itself, does not bring Lane's speech within the protection of the First Amendment," the court ruled.

Today the U.S. Supreme Court will hear arguments on the Lane case. It will consider whether the government "is categorically free under the First Amendment to retaliate against a public employee for truthful sworn testimony that was compelled by subpoena and wasn't a part of the employee's ordinary job responsibilities; and whether qualified immunity precludes a claim for damages in such an act."

It is billed as a case important to whistleblowers' rights. But in reality, it is important for simple common sense.

Because being a public employee does not make you immune from being a citizen.

Being a public employee should not make you reluctant to take the stand in the interest of justice, to tell the truth and the whole truth and nothing but the truth.

Being a public employee should not make you have to choose between honesty and job security.

One should never be fired for telling the truth.

There is no telling what the U.S. Supreme Court will decide on this issue. It will take weeks and this Court's interpretations of free speech have been ... broad.

It ought to be simpler than this. Too bad there's not a common sense clause in the Constitution.

John Archibald is a columnist for Alabama Media Group. jarchibald@al.com

Do the right thing, Alabama, and give whistleblower Edward Lane the job he earned

By John Archibald
jarchibald@al.com
AL.com Opinion

The U.S. Supreme Court this week rightly sided with Alabama whistleblower Edward Lane, a rare former employee of the two-year college system who refused to ignore corruption and business as usual.

Lane ran a program at Central Alabama Community College a few years ago. And trouble started when he demanded to know what a former legislator (Rep. Sue Schmitz, who would later go to jail) did in her double-dipping two-year college job. He found out she did pretty much nothing.

He fired her. He testified – after being subpoenaed – against her.

There were threats and offers and warnings. And in the end he lost his job and his career.

He has thought about it a lot since it all came down in 2009. He has no doubt he'd be sitting pretty in a posh office right now if he had heeded the warnings and turned a blind eye.

But his parents taught him better than that, he said. His religion demands more.

"Not doing the right thing was never an option," he said this week. "I knew what I faced."

So he has been left to find work where he could. He's happy and grateful to be a security guard in Anniston, he says, but not so happy to bring home a third of the pay he used to earn.

But this week all nine members of the High Court agreed that he got the shaft. The justices agreed that the First Amendment protects public employees who provide "truthful sworn testimony, compelled by a subpoena."

A picture with my Wife Sena Lane and my Son Evan Lane taken April 28, 2014 inside the Supreme Court while waiting to be seated for Oral Arguments of my case Lane V. Franks

The problem is that the win doesn't really help Lane out. He still lost his job. The two-year system says the job doesn't exist anymore, because they dismantled it to make sure. It will help people in Lane's position in the future, but not Lane himself.

So every lawyer is talking about the next steps. Fighting for jobs and defending the state and ...*No Mas!*

Stop it. It's time for Alabama to show a little appreciation. It's time for Alabama to give this guy a job.

Don't tell me his job doesn't exist. This is a system that found jobs for a third of all state legislators before Lane and others helped put a few away. If he was a politician they'd find a way.

If his old job doesn't exist, find another one.

Watchdog in chief, maybe, or head of the department of honest-to-God ethics. The guy has a history in corrections, a master's degree and a history of doing all the things we want our public officials to do.

Like the right thing.

What about us?

The governor is by virtue his office the head of the Alabama Board of Education. He could make it happen, if he wanted.

He was swept into power, recall, on a wave of revulsion for the type of corruption that Lane himself pointed out. So was Attorney General Luther Strange, who campaigned on a platform of cleaning up corruption.

It's not enough to say the First Amendment should protect a guy like Lane, and then walk away.

We need to keep him, to reward him in the same way we reward everyone who does a good job in the face of tremendous pressure to do a bad one.

Lane said he would like to come to an agreement. But then he laughed.

"I don't know if they would want me hanging around," he said. "My way of thinking is we're going to do the right thing or we're not going to do it at all."

Which is exactly why Alabama ought to do the right thing. Tell the lawyers to shut up. Don't just give him a job. Give him back what he earned.

John Archibald is a columnist for Alabama Media Group. jarchibald@al.com

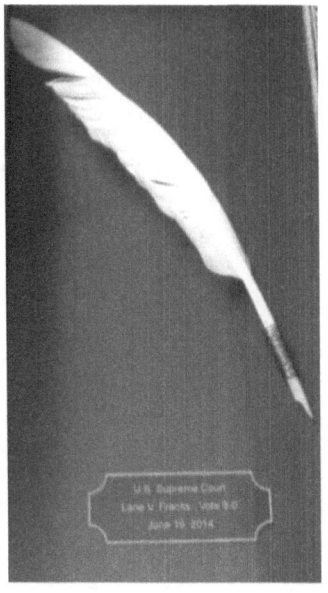

A unique tradition maintained since the earliest sessions of the Supreme Court is the presenting of goose-feather pens to advocates who appear for oral argument. The practice reportedly dates back to the early 1800s, when Chief Justice John Marshall provided lawyers with quill pens to take notes. The quill pen is a cherished memento of an appearance before the Supreme Court.

SCOTUS Blog

SUPREME COURT OF THE UNITED STATES BLOG

Lane v. Franks
Docket No. 13-483

Disclosure: Goldstein & Russell, P.C., whose attorneys contribute to this blog in various capacities, serves as counsel to the petitioner in this case.

Holding: Testimony in a criminal prosecution by a government employee about fraud in the program where he works is protected by the First Amendment; however, the supervisor who fired him in retaliation for that testimony has qualified immunity from suit because it wasn't "beyond debate" that the employee's testimony was protected.

Judgment: Affirmed in part, reversed in part, and remanded., 9-0, in an opinion by Justice Sotomayor on June 19, 2014.

SCOTUSblog Coverage

- Commentary: The fundamental constitutional principle not discussed in *Lane v. Franks* (Marty Lederman)
- Opinion analysis: First Amendment clearly protects public employee's subpoenaed testimony – but not sufficiently clearly to overcome qualified immunity (Ruthann Robson)
- Argument analysis: How wrong was the Eleventh Circuit about the First Amendment protections for a public employee's subpoenaed testimony? (Ruthann Robson)
- Argument preview: First Amendment protections for public employee's subpoenaed testimony (Ruthann Robson)
- SCOTUS for law students (sponsored by Bloomberg Law): Qualified immunity (Stephen Wermiel)
- Court to rule on cellphone privacy (Lyle Denniston)
- Petition of the day (Mary Pat Dwyer)

Date	Proceedings and Orders
Oct 15	Petition for a writ of certiorari filed.

2013		(Response due November 18, 2013)
Nov 2013	14	Brief of respondent Steve Franks in opposition filed.
Nov 2013	26	Reply of petitioner Edward R. Lane filed.
Dec 2013	4	DISTRIBUTED for Conference of January 10, 2014.
Jan 2014	13	DISTRIBUTED for Conference of January 17, 2014.
Jan 2014	17	Petition GRANTED.
Feb 2014	4	Consent to the filing of amicus curiae briefs, in support of either party or of neither party, received from counsel for the petitioner.
Feb 2014	11	SET FOR ARGUMENT ON Monday, April 28, 2014
Feb 2014	19	Consent to the filing of amicus curiae briefs, in support of either party or of neither party, received from counsel for the respondent Steve Franks.

Feb 20 2014		Consent to the filing of amicus curiae briefs, in support of either party or of neither party, received from counsel for the respondent Susan Burrows.
Feb 20 2014		Motion to dispense with printing the joint appendix filed by petitioner Edward R. Lane.
Mar 3 2014		Brief of petitioner Edward R. Lane filed.
Mar 3 2014		Brief of respondent Susan Burrow in support of reversal in part and affirmance in part filed.
Mar 5 2014		Brief amicus curiae of Alliance Defending Freedom filed.
Mar 7 2014		Brief amicus curiae of National Whistleblower Center filed. (Distributed)
Mar 10 2014		Motion to dispense with printing the joint appendix filed by petitioner GRANTED.
Mar 10 2014		Record received from U.S.D.C. Northern District of Alabama is

		electronic. (Not on PACER).
Mar 2014		CIRCULATED.
Mar 2014	10	Brief amici curiae of American Civil Liberties Union, et al. filed. (Distributed)
Mar 2014	10	Brief amici curiae of Law Professors filed. (Distributed)
Mar 2014	10	Brief amicus curiae of Government Accountability Project filed. (Distributed)
Mar 2014	10	Brief amicus curiae of United States supporting affirmance in part and reversal in part filed.
Mar 2014	10	Brief amicus curiae of The National Association of Police Organizations filed. (Distributed)
Mar 2014	10	Brief amici curiae of National Education Association, et al. filed. (Distributed)
Mar 2014	10	Brief amicus curiae of First Amendment Coalition filed.

		(Distributed)
Mar 10 2014		Brief amicus curiae of American Federation of Labor and Congress of Industrial Organizations filed. (Distributed)
Apr 2 2014		Brief of respondent Steve Franks filed. (Distributed)
Apr 8 2014		Motion of the Solicitor General for leave to participate in oral argument as amicus curiae, for divided argument, and for allocation of argument time filed.
Apr 9 2014		Brief amici curiae of The International Municipal Lawyers Association, et al. filed. (Distributed)
Apr 11 2014		Reply of petitioner Edward R. Lane filed. (Distributed)
Apr 17 2014		Reply of respondent Susan Burrow filed. (Distributed)
Apr 18 2014		Motion of the Solicitor General for leave to participate in oral argument as amicus curiae, for

		divided argument, and for allocation of argument time GRANTED.
Apr 2014	22	Letter from counsel for petitioner Edward R. Lane filed. (Distributed)
Apr 2014	28	Argued. For petitioner: Tejinder Singh, Washington, D. C.; and Ian H. Gershengorn, Deputy Solicitor General, Department of Justice, Washington, D. C. (for United States, as amicus curiae.) For respondent Burrow: Luther J. Strange, III, Attorney General, Montgomery, Ala. For respondent Franks: Mark T. Waggoner, Birmingham, Ala.
Jun 2014	19	Adjudged to be AFFIRMED IN PART, REVERSED IN PART, and case REMANDED. Sotomayor, J., delivered the opinion for a unanimous Court. Thomas, J., filed a concurring opinion, in which Scalia and Alito, JJ., joined.
Jul 2014	21	JUDGMENT ISSUED

John D. Saxon | Employment, Discrimination & Civil Rights Attorney 2119 3rd Ave N, Birmingham, AL 35203. I have to thank my Attorney John Saxon the Alabama Education Association (AEA) and the National Education Association (NEA) for standing by me and representing me after I was terminated from my job with the State of Alabama. Attorney Saxon worked to get my case into federal court when the odds were totally against me. He truly fights for the rights of the people he represents and in my case it was certainly a David versus Goliath but he and his Law firm stepped up and represented me.

www.ingramcontent.com/pod-product-compliance
Lightning Source LLC
Chambersburg PA
CBHW032047290426
44110CB00012B/988